Heartworm
the ramblings of a 20-something

Teri M. Dawson

The right of Teri M. Dawson to be identified
as the author, illustrator and designer has been
asserted in accordance with the
Copyright, Designs and
Patents Act 1988.

ALL RIGHTS RESERVED

No part of this publication may be reproduced, stored
in a retrieval system, or transmitted, in any form or by
any means (electronic, mechanical, photocopying,
recording or otherwise), without the prior written
permission of the publisher.

Printed in the United Kingdom
First Printing, 2021

ISBN: Print (Hard Cover):
978-1-8383723-7-8

Published by Purple Parrot Publishing
www.purpleparrotpublishing.co.uk

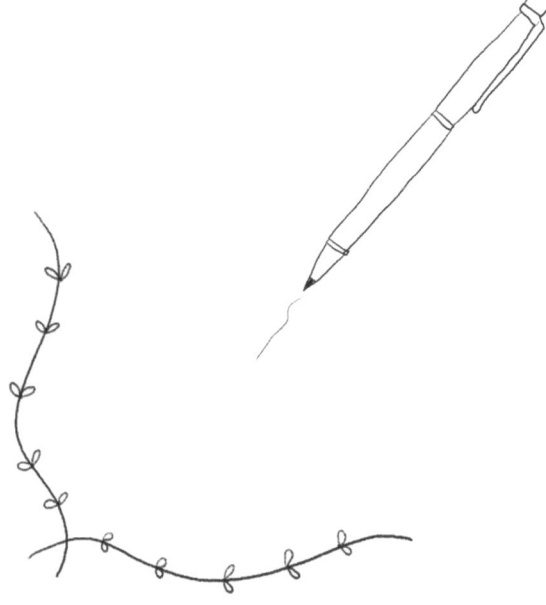

To Mum, for always reading.

To Dad, for introducing me to
Leonard Cohen.

To Bella, for being the best sister.

To Kirsty, Leanne, Helen, Hannah,
Lyndsey and Amy, for being the
best friends I could ask for.

To Yvonne, Kat and Neil, for all of the
help and support.

To those that inspired these
ramblings, for being a part
of my life and my past.

To Mike, for everything.

Rae

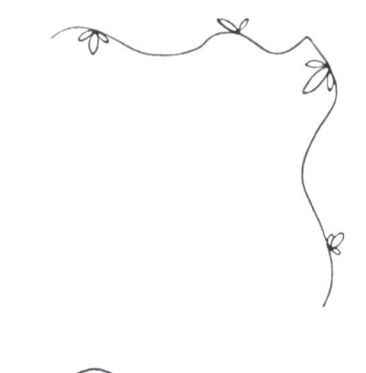

She spoke on the radio
of this time last year;
of the rust and the algae
beneath the North Pier,
the smell of burnt sugar
and sun-faded souvenirs.

So you turned up the volume -
remembering her curly hair
and how you'd get to school early
every morning
just to spend more time
alone with her.

Then, no direction,
you said that we'd just drive -
but you followed the signs
to her hometown
and we arrived just in time
to walk along the waterside
at low tide.

But I wore the wrong shoes,
I don't do much right.

She can be your Daisy,
I'll be your Green Light.

Swinging

If I remember anything
about tonight,
I hope it's the way
that I felt like Lux Lisbon
when I swung too high,

because the sunlight
seeped through the
leaves and grazed my eyes

and that's what
Jeffrey would have wanted
even though I'm not blonde,
and my bed never had a
canopy to hang my
rebellion on,

and we don't ever get fish flies
where I come from,
and I've got the correct amount of
teeth in my mouth.

And how strange it had
seemed to me
that I should feel like her,

when it was Bonnie
who swung from the rope,

and it's Therese
whose name I almost share.

Untitled

You hear the words
in my handwriting
echo off the page.

I hear the words,
in the front seat;
your father's
hand-me-down
rage.

Bone Marrow

I remember her sitting
on the edge of the sink,
and she said she must love him
because she could feel it
in her bone marrow;

I've always loved how poetic
she gets when she drinks.

Haiku No 1.

A picture of me
taking a picture of you.
Did you keep it safe?

Untitled

no
is
a full
sentence

Boosh

I was so excited
to tell everyone
at school

that I'd been to
see them
live
on
tour.

I thought it
made me cool.

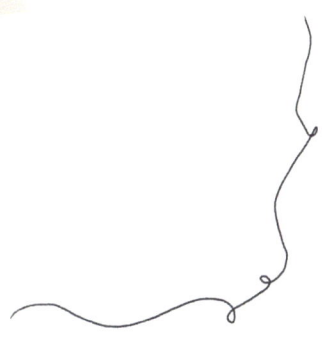

July 19th, Your Red Car

We were both almost grown
and your hair was gone;

I laughed
because I'd never seen
your forehead before.

With you I was
Jane,
Awake again,

because we drove
to a new place
before all the old ones,

past our old school
then down Dagger Lane
in the fog, at midnight,
when I had work the next day.

And I'll remember
that night,
after the turn
in your mind,

because I
spoke of the scars
on another
man's thighs

and it was only
for looking
that I saw
the trouble
I'd left for
safekeeping
somewhere
in your eyes.

Haiku No 2.

Driving in your car
makes me feel like a grown up.
We're going too fast.

Untitled

We think that
the six of us
will always be
this way.

We're
too young
to see the things
that time
can take
away.

Vinyl Lullabies

Corner store whisky,
we slept on the living room floor.

It surprised me,
you were funny -

you always looked so serious
before.

That night it snowed;
1am, your scarf,
bottle cap for a nose.

Tiptoe around the garden;
the city sleeps
and time slows.

Drop the needle,
red wine,
lean back,
close your eyes.

Sleeping in your Levi's
with your vinyl lullabies.

Haiku No. 3

I only called you
twenty seven times today.
Guess I'm moving on.

Zodiac Lines

The words you scatter set the room aglow;
fallen sparks upon the carpet dance,
you draw me in, then let me go.

Enraptured by the seeds you sow -
of this one night of happenstance.
The words you scatter set the room aglow.

To keep me still is all you know,
to hold my secrets in your glance.
You draw me in, then let me go.

You tell me you're a Scorpio,
so to excuse you in advance.
The words you scatter set the room aglow.

Lose yourself in the afterglow
of your failed attempts at past romance.
You draw me in, then let me go.

You wear this sadness just for show;
the bruises your ego enhance.
The words you scatter set the room aglow,
you draw me in, then let me go.

The Fall

The taste of early October
freckled my lower lip
through an open bus window
beside a building site
and, for some reason,
it reminded me of your
kitchen.

And of the broken beams
on your stairwell,
your neighbour's gate
creaking in the winter
and Bernard Black mornings
with scrambled eggs

and the coffee thing.
The cigarette thing.
The garden shoes and
stolen QE2 bathrobe thing.
The polite cat on the footpath thing.
The royal blue turned up collar thing.
And it's easier to do this
if I pretend I was just your
summer girl;

it's really not your fault that you
found me in the spring.

And we would never have made it
to the Cotswolds on a bicycle,
or found time for
the "picnic on the Guild Wheel" thing.

It seems that I know
how to be outside,
after all,

And I was just your summer girl,
so you ditched me
in the fall.

Maggie

I remember the way
in her saddle shoes
she sat;

Mr Moonlight
beneath her tongue
and swinging slowly
on a children's park
for the last hour,
burnt amber,
of an early March evening.

And how she had smiled;

eyes closed,
mind open.

Heartworm

I liked the word
(at first)
because the shape
that my mouth made
when I repeated it
suggested that I could
have used it as an insult,
and that I'd appear
refined
and well-read
to those who heard it
at a quick (note; strategic)
speed

(because, unsure of definition,
I'd have said it quickly
with no desire to mislead).

I know there's much
to be said
about those
with graces and airs,
so for occasions
such as these
I keep a dictionary
in the airing cupboard
at the top of the stairs;

```
refulgent

re·ful·gent

adj.

Shining radiantly; resplendent.
```

and I thought the word
to be lovely,
and a little nebulous

(which is, by chance,
another word that I like
the sound of -
if only because it defines
not a cloud of dust.)

That was on a Thursday,
which are a little different
for me now –
because I don't take a bus
past your work
every morning anymore,

or feel comforted
(almost wanted,
consoled,
accounted for)
by the pungent
(but not unwelcome)
7am petrichor.

I suppose what I'm saying
is that words don't always
mean what they appear to.

So I'll call you a heartworm;

I know that you'll
find something
in that definition
to adhere to.

Grapefruit

Is there still
a hole
in the door
to your bedroom?

Does your
mum
still buy
the best
bread?

Does the
portrait
of your
summer
in Whitby

still hang
on the wall
overhead?

Do your
baby shoes
still sit
on the
mantel

painted
gold,
in a row
with your
sisters'?

Do you
still think
about
grapefruit
in the caravan?

Did your heart
ever heal
from the blisters?

Lip Balm

Rest our heads on green elbows, dew-damp grass.
It's not like us to keep skipping class but
we stayed up late and slept through our alarm.
Sunburnt noses; you borrow my lip-balm.

Haiku No. 4

I lost my ticket.
Could you maybe drive me home?
See - we are still friends.

Annie

I see your other
lovers,
they pass me
in the streets;

hollow eyes,
skinny thighs,
swollen cheeks.

I feel like
I can't do this
on my own.

Annie,
won't you
please
come
home?

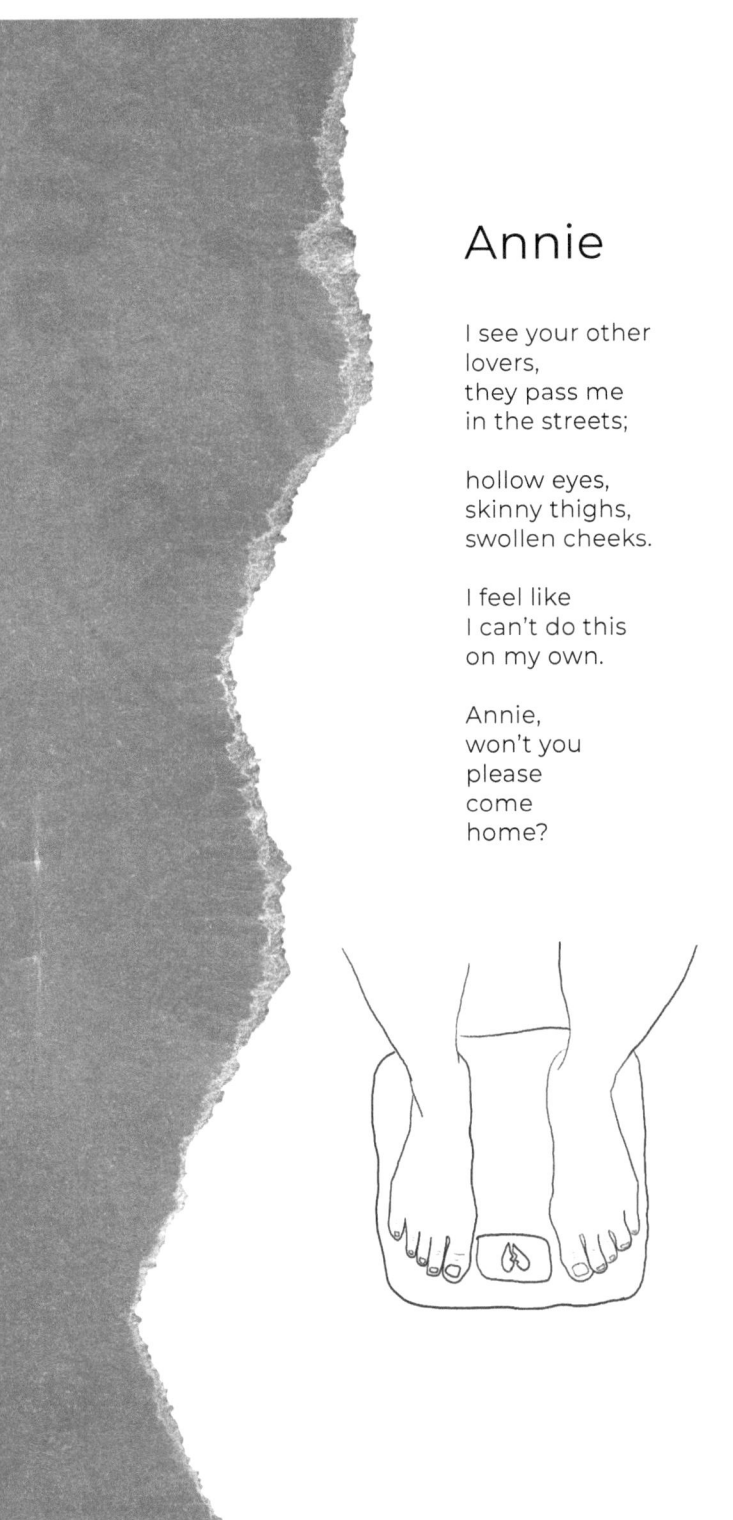

Celeste

Oh,
sweet girl.

How could he
do that
to you?

Cramp

I learned to run
without moving my feet.

I memorised the steps
to my house
from your street.

The years ran by, too,
and they led me astray.

Another face
on the terrace
watching me run away.

My name in black ink;
no address, no stamp.

I tried to stay still
but your words
gave me cramp.

We started again,
just to turn on a dime.

My heart is restless;
she runs
all the time.

Lost

I know that somewhere,

your life is playing out
in the window
of a house

with a door number
that I don't know.

And I hope that you're happy,
wherever you are.

Wake

Nobody else can tell you
how to shape the things you see,
the same world that made me careful
has made you so carefree.

I was so busy keeping quiet
while you set this town aglow;
that's how I became a breeze
and you became a tornado.

But if all we make are choices
and all we have is all we take,
it shouldn't matter what our gale-force
for we should all leave something in our wake.

The Last Time

I arrived at 9,
I left at 2,
and who should I meet
in the doorway
but you?

You arrived at 2,
You left at 9,
spilling out into the morning
with breath like red wine.

I'm always leaving
just as you arrive
and that,

my dear,

is why we

didn't survive.

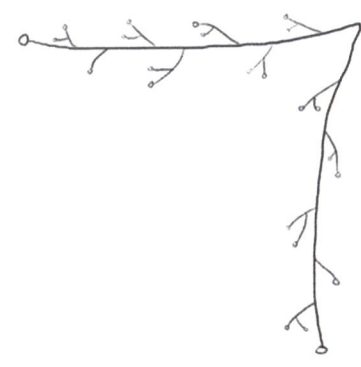

Haiku No. 5

It's cold here tonight –
reminds me of your bedroom.
Windows wide open.

The Week We Shared

I wonder who
you could have been.

Would you have sunburned
as easily as me?

I'm sure you would
have liked it here.

13

The sidelines of
the basketball court,
my pink MP3 player.

We tried,
I suppose.

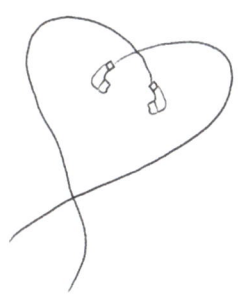

Dressing Gown

I knew you
inside out.

Now I don't even know
where you live.

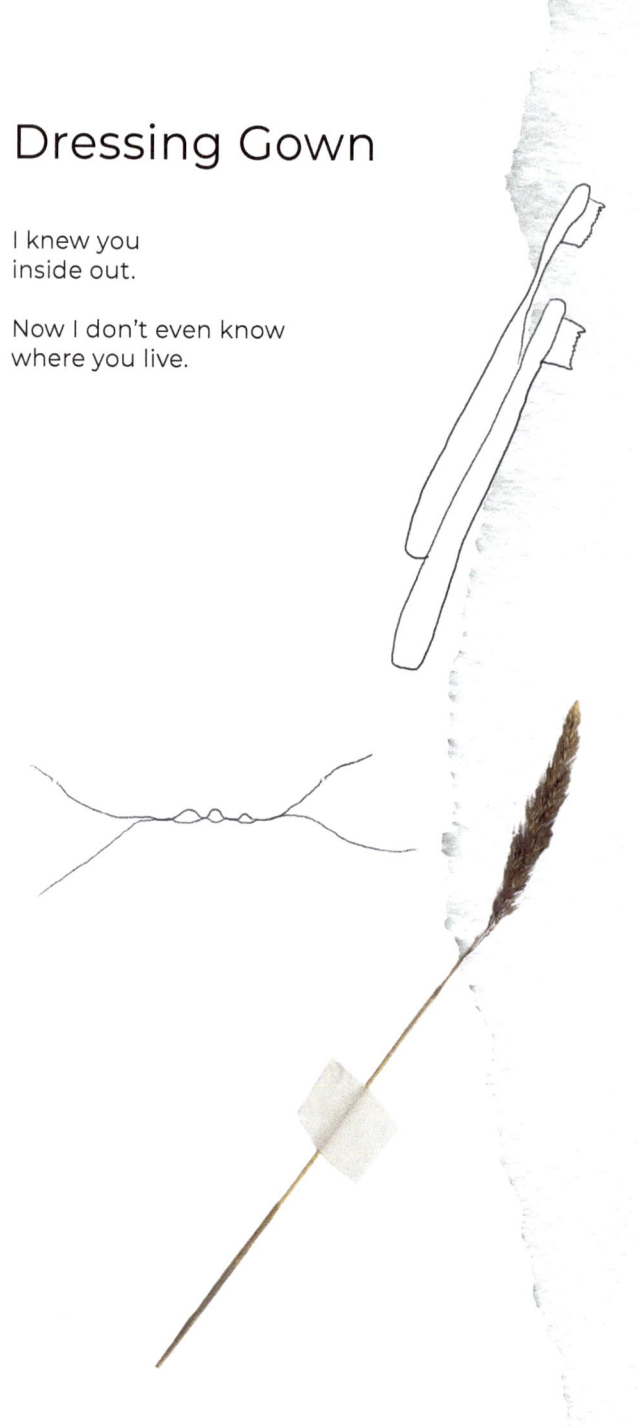

Unititled

I see you there,
swaying in the crowd.

Swallows dance
along your neckline

and I wonder
who loves you now.

Haiku No. 6

A thousand wishes,
and if only one came true
I'd still have you here.

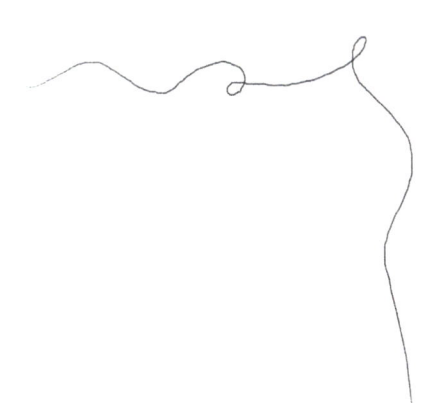

T.S.

She's putting
a lot
of
new music
out
lately.

I'm sorry
if it all
reminds
you
of me.

You

I lost the life
I searched for,
found you etched
upon the map -

the veins of my city
dance, entangled,
around your neck

but

your wicked mind,
I've come to find,
will lead me nowhere
worth the drive.

I lost my love
amidst the downpour,
lost my youth
in my protests;

all the good ones
getting older,
losing dreams to suits
and paint-scuffed desks.

I won't be young
forever;
won't be wild,
beguiled
and free.

I'll be the hill
you'll gladly die on
and I'll break your heart
so gently.

I'll dance
this lonely tango,
tangled up
in all things new -

but when the rain
clears away the thunder
I know all I'll see
is you.

Untitled

Young bones,
old soul.

Give me the world,
I'll swallow it whole.

Ovary Acting

I wish you worked
the way
you were
supposed to.

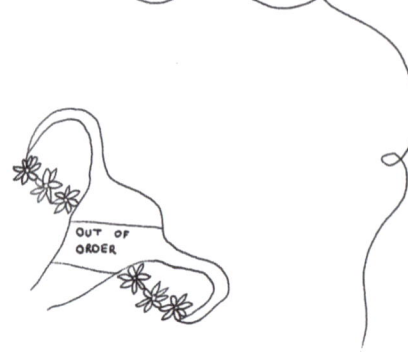

Ramblings

To understand words,
to transcribe and start fires,
you must have more than
infrequent desire,

and so much more than
a pen and a style,
more than the urge
every once in a while
to think back on memories
and tinker with rhyme -
more than a longing
that's distant with time.

More than torment
under your tongue
and more than a life
that isn't lifelong.
More than wisdom
unburdened by age
and more than those
with whom you
shared the stage.

To write what's worth reading
try to understand more
than the ramblings of those
who rambled before.

And what if we want
all our pain to lie dormant?

How much must we suffer
before we can write
something
important?

I Always Do

It sounds like Eric Church
with the windows rolled down,
like low-lying sunshine
as we drive through my hometown.

Like sunglasses on your head,
like mud stains on your jeans,
like smiling in the summertime
like lovesick, boundless teens.

Tomorrow we'll feel older
beneath that Georgia moon,
but for now let's just be seventeen
driving around all afternoon.

I recognise the sound of it,
just like I always do.
You see, it's like a country song
whenever I'm with you.

2021

I miss my friends.

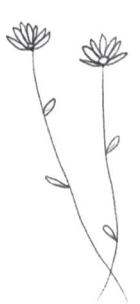

Dark Outside

I've always liked riding
the bus at night
in the rain.

There's something about
the neon glow of the lights
that we pass,

and the way that
the bus interior
reflects itself
in all of the windows

that just makes me
feel so safe.

I feel the same way
about supermarkets
at night

and petrol stations.

Maybe I just enjoy
being near people
when it's dark outside.

Kirsty

He'd be so proud
to see you now;

his little girl
with a girl
of her own.

Honeycomb

Leather seat,
burning heat.

Summer dress,
bare feet.

Smile at me,
drive me home.

Your shirt smells
like honeycomb.

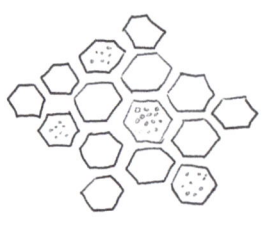

Untitled

The
day
I
agreed
to
a
new
surname.

Hard Times

Sammy sits at the counter,
a double whisky for the road.
He sees the pale grey eyes
of the barmaid pulling pints
and thinks of his girl back home.

He counts the change
through his front pocket,
prays for the outline of a bill.
It's just another Tuesday night
at The Hard Times Bar and Grill.

Sammy had it good once,
a couple kids, a house, a wife,
but he was no stranger to
the harder times in life.

He fell back on bad habits,
thought he understood the game.
Now he drifts along the railway,
a couple twenties to his name.

Winona takes her hair down,
counts the tips left in the jar.
When did her whole life become
this run down, broken bar?

A couple short,
he'll catch her next time.
She takes their word,
they take their fill.
It's just another Tuesday night
at The Hard Times Bar and Grill.

Winona's pretty face
was once enough to get her by.
Said she was gonna be a movie star
but never had the guts to try.

Now her face reads like a roadmap,
lines that lead her from her dreams.
She was only supposed stay the summer
when she started work here in her teens.

In any other bar,
in any other town,
they'd strike up a conversation,
maybe find some common ground.

But tonight, he'll call it quits -
give up hope of a refill.
He'll stumble out into the winter night
and barely feel the icy chill.

And she'll wipe down the counter,
top up the morning's coffee mill.

She'll dream tomorrow will be better,
oh, one day it surely will.

Because she can't have peaked already,
can't be heading straight downhill.

Or worse,
be standing still.

Everyone's favourite barmaid
wears a smile all day until

the end of another Tuesday night
at The Hard Times Bar and Grill.

Hiraeth

It was not nostalgia I felt
when I heard the news,
because I never knew you
though I knew your face
and name,

I knew you came
from Vojvodina
though that wasn't
where you found
your fame.

I knew about
the $50 in your father's
wallet; of the year 2000
in New York City with only
what you could fit
inside your tiny pockets.

And I see your face
behind my eyelids
as both a blonde
and a brunette

which is a strange
thing to do of someone
I have never met.

It was almost nostalgia I
felt on Sunday;
homesickness
for a place I'd
never visited nor
left behind.

I'll borrow
a word, Hiraeth -
it's the closest
definition I can find.

I'm Sure I Didn't Make You Up

In daylight, you're the whimsy I have to dismiss
because you withered away upon weary eyes awoken,
and in the morning your absence leaves nothing amiss.

In dreams, all things out of sight are half broken
or hollow, unglued memories of the day -
and the words I remember were surely never spoken.

Soon I'll replace you, you'll drift or decay
as I once again lay my head down to rest,
and another will seep in softly as you fade away.

16

You're only sixteen;
there's so much yet to see.

Reading John Green,
you're only sixteen;
laughing in the canteen,
not sure yet who you'll be.

You're only sixteen;
there's so much yet to see.

Untitled

Like

smoke,

you

cling

to

everything.

This Night

It's not the dark that scares me,
it's what cannot be seen.
It's doors I've never walked through
not the places that I've been -
it's the fear of the obscene.

Strain my neck beyond the light
and face, head on, the unforeseen;
the dark will force me to be bright.
I'll find my own way through this night.

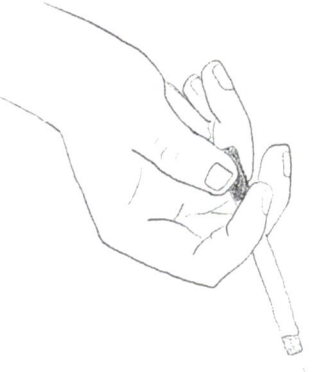

Doorstep

You light up a cigarette
on the doorstep, midnight air.
A week in, so I don't know you yet.

You light up a cigarette,
I'm trying not to look upset -
your closed mind is elsewhere.

You light up a cigarette
on the doorstep, midnight air.

Plague

You'd play my guitar,
I'd play with your spine;
play games in the
dreamscape you'd
made in my mind.

And then, a Tuesday,
November 18th;
my first day of training
and the last time I'd eat

for a while.

You arrived
empty handed -
no petrol station
Cola to place,
half-drunk
on the living room
table and

you said your
sister had already
known; she's seen
you get tangled
in wanting to
want things.

You've known
since fourteen -
you don't
want this at all.

I always thought
I'd be easier to love
when there was less
of me,

so now I count
everything -
even the teaspoon
of milk in my coffee.

I'll throw away
old clothes
because they
don't fit me,

or because I have
one less reason now
for long sleeves.

You keep lines blurry,
endearments are vague -

remember the way,
smelling like pepper,
said you'd made a mistake;

"Babe - I can't change.
One man's discomfort
is another man's plague."

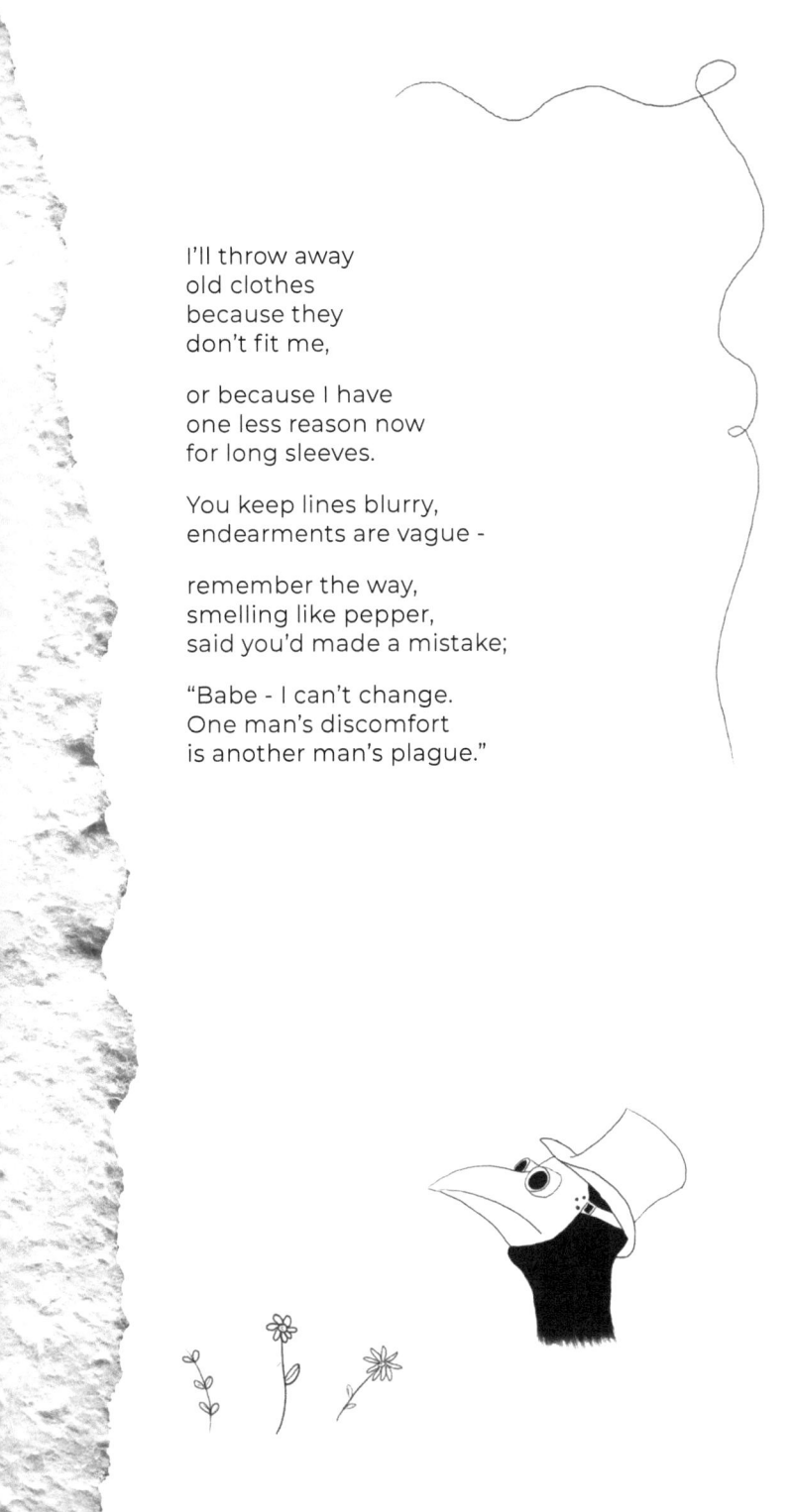

The Ending

Old Mr Marvin was a peculiar man,
he owned a bookshop down on Timon Lane.
From the outside, it appeared like any other place;
the kind that you'd browse as you sheltered from rain.

But Mr Marvin's inventory was a curious kind;
his books left the reader with a taste bittersweet.
For Mr Marvin had spent his life filling these shelves
with stories aplenty - but each left incomplete.

Some interrupted by untimely misfortune,
others neglected; cast-off by design.
Some abandoned for passions anew,
and others simply never given the time.

One day, amidst a most raucous downpour,
in swept young Melody - her plans gone awry.
She was warming her hands by the log-burning fire
when, covered in cobwebs, a book caught her eye.

As she leafed through the pages, her mind took a journey
with a handsome young prince and a beautiful maid.
The rain turned to drizzle, but the lady - enraptured -
approached Mr Marvin at the till and she paid.

The next morning, a frantic and weary Miss Melody
swept in, rather bothered, through the bookshop's front door;
"Mr Marvin" she gasped, her voice all a quiver,
"This book ends abruptly on page 94!"

He smiled at the young woman's clear confusion;
"Yes my dear, that is part of the fun!
The stories I house here weren't given their endings,
still I wanted to allow them their day in the sun."

But Miss Melody was a headstrong, determined young lady,
and she begged him to find what she so dearly sought.
So the old man agreed that he'd search for the ending
though he knew that the chances he'd find it were nought.

Though at first she'd visit him most every morning,
over time her calls grew ever sporadic.
Miss Melody feared that she may never know
what became of The Maid and The Royal Romantic.

It was many years later, she flicked through the paper;
her children at school, her eyes wrinkled by age.
She was all but done reading, when at once she saw
Mr Marvin's obituary staring up from the page.

The bookshop was open for one more day only;
that old place she'd once called at every day.
Without even thinking she pulled on her coat,
picked up her umbrella and set off on her way.

It seemed like a lifetime since last she had been there,
yet not much had changed in that little bookshop.
She meandered the aisles before finding an envelope -
the words, "The Ending", were scrawled on the top.

With trembling hands and eyes growing misty,
she carefully pulled out the letter inside.
Could this be the ending she'd desperately searched for,
yet long ago given up hope that she'd find?

"Melody, I hope that this letter soon finds you.
Please forgive me, I know this has taken so long.
Dearest friend, I hope that by now you can see it -
how the ending has been inside you all along.

For you never doubted that the prince find his way,
he was always to be with the maid he loved dearly.
Why did you need another to confirm
what you already knew in your heart so clearly?

We don't need another's approval, old friend,
for we alone choose what our ending shall be.
So, dearest Melody, choose yours well;
for only you can preface your ending with 'happy'".

From that day onwards Miss Melody knew
that she alone had the power to win or to lose.
She made it her mission to end all things wisely
so, Dear Reader, which one will you chose?

www.ingramcontent.com/pod-product-compliance
Lightning Source LLC
Chambersburg PA
CBHW042259280426
43661CB00098BA/1187